GOOD CENT$

A Simple Budget for Christian Young People

Ed Murrell

CROSSBOOKS
PUBLISHING

CrossBooks™
A Division of LifeWay
1663 Liberty Drive
Bloomington, IN 47403
www.crossbooks.com
Phone: 1-866-879-0502

First published by CrossBooks 5/28/2010

ISBN: 978-1-6150-7206-4 (sc)

Library of Congress Control Number: 2010905769

Printed in the United States of America
Bloomington, Indiana

This book is printed on acid-free paper.

"I hate money, but it soothes my nerves." *
Joe Louis

"That money talks
I'll not deny
I heard it once
It said 'Goodbye'" **
Richard Armour

"Debt is where you tell God you love Him and you want to live for Him and let Him lead you through this life – then you go out and spend more money than He has given you."
Ed Murrell

"If you want to be excellent at something, live on a budget. By living on a budget you will be excellent in your personal finances. No matter how average you think you are at everything else, you can be excellent in your personal finances by simply living on a budget."
Ed Murrell

Hello,

My name is Ed Murrell and I have developed the Good Cent$ Budget to help young people like you avoid the miserable financial mess I got myself into back when I was young.

To make your learning a little easier, most of the information will be presented in "bullet" form. It is my hope that this will help you remember what you learn within these pages.

All through this book you will be challenged with questions. Take your time and answer each one of them carefully. Don't worry, the questions are not difficult. They are there just to help you remember and fully understand what you learn.

At the end of the book you will find pages where you can figure your budgets, list all of your debts, write down your saving goals, and keep a journal of your progress during your first year on The Good Cent$ Budget.

Please read the entire book before you plan your budget.

As you read Good Cent$ and start your budget, please feel free to email goodcentsbudget@yahoo.com if you have any questions. I will answer your email as quickly as I can.

I hope you enjoy learning about the Good Cent$ budget and I hope it will be a blessing to your life.

God bless you.

CONTENTS

1
MY STORY

From Nonsense to Good Cent$

One day in May 1989, I counted up all of my debts and was shocked to find that I owed $45,000 to various creditors ($15,000 on a new Chevy Scottsdale pick-up truck, $3,000 to the IRS, and $27,000 in unsecured credit card debt). By today's standards that may not seem like a lot, but at the time my struggling landscaping business was bringing in an annual income of less than $20,000. I might as well have owed 45 *million* dollars.

I felt defeated and depressed. Collectors called constantly. Thank goodness I didn't have a cell phone then, or I might have gone completely crazy. My financial problems affected every area of my life in a negative way. One collector told me, "Murrell, you're a disgrace. You can't even pay your bills. People like you make me sick." I hated hearing that, but I had no money and a ton of debt. How could I argue with the guy?

How did my life get like this? Well, my pathetic story begins back when I was a kid going to school. The basic subjects were taught well enough, but there was absolutely no teaching on personal finances – none in elementary school, none in junior high, and none in high school. Even in college, I received no teaching on personal finances.

I grew up in a big family. My dear old dad used to tell people, "I have six sons and each one has two sisters". People would respond in near horror. My dad would laugh and tell them, "Relax! They each have the same two sisters. We *only* have eight kids."

Coming from a family that size was great fun. I never felt a lack of friends because I had quite a few friends at home. Of course these "friends" were also my fellow competitors for our parent's time. It was very difficult for my parents to cover all the bases with every kid. They were good role models, and they did a great job raising us, but they didn't teach us a lot about personal finances.

They did teach us one thing, though; they paid cash for almost everything. Think about that; eight kids, a house, a car, Catholic schools, etc. and they paid cash for almost everything. Amazing discipline! They handled money the right way and we kids saw them doing that. I wish that modeled lesson would have penetrated my brain a little deeper than it did.

Growing up Catholic was great. The Church taught me a lot about life and God and loving Him and my fellow man, but I can't ever remember hearing a sermon on personal finances. More than two thousand Bible verses deal with money, but the Church didn't teach the subject.

With very little teaching on finances at home and no teaching at all on the subject at school or church, it was just a matter of time before I would make a serious financial mistake. I remember the day it happened very well. I was walking toward an auditorium at South Texas Jr. College in downtown Houston, where I was a first year student, when I heard a guy yell out, "Hey, chief, how about coming over here and opening up a department store credit card account? It only takes a few minutes".

At first I was not sure he was talking to me, but he soon let me know he was. "Come on, man, you need this. It's financial freedom." He wouldn't shut up, "It only takes a few minutes, man. This will help you start establishing a credit history. Then you can get more cards and, man, it just keeps on growing."

I guess I was frowning or something; maybe because credit and credit cards were still foreign to me. Maybe I knew deep down that there was danger here with this hyperactive credit card salesman. Anyway, he must have felt I was too cautious because he started in on me again, "Man, with this card you can get in on sales even if you're short on cash at the time. And listen, it is just cool to be able to whip out a credit card when you want to buy something."

I should have run away from that sales table as fast as I could, but I didn't. I lingered and listened to more hype. Then I took a wrong turn in my life. I signed a piece of paper saying I wanted a credit card. Stupid, stupid, stupid!!!

In a few minutes I went to class. In a few days the department store credit card table was gone. In a few weeks, I received my brand new credit card in the mail. In a few months, I was in debt. In a few years, debt had stalled my life. If only I would have had Good Cent$ back then, my life might have been easier.

After using the card a few times, I received my first statement and was happy to see that, although I had charged $240, I only had to make a minimum payment of $10 for that month. The next month I charged another $50 and still only had to pay $10 for that month. Wow! What a deal!

Soon after, I received an application for another department store card in the mail. By now I was liking this credit card thing, so I filled out the application and mailed it back. Bingo! I was accepted. Now I had *two* credit cards.

The first card had a credit limit of $500 and I was almost there. My plan was to begin paying that card off and use the second card for purchases. Great plan except I soon maxed out the second card without paying down the first one at all. I was just a few months into my credit card career and I already had $1,200 worth of debt at an average interest rate of 11.9 percent. (The rate would be a lot higher today.) In my utter brilliance, I decided that the way out of this was to get more cards.

I quickly amassed $5,000 in credit card debt. Eventually, I applied for and was approved for a Master Card. Now I could charge anything, anytime, anywhere. When my total debt reached $10,000 I began to struggle to make the minimum payments. When the minimum payments no longer covered the monthly interest, I was sunk. I had too much debt and not enough income.

By the time I was twenty six years old I found my first gray hair.

To add to my problems, I bought a truck in 1975 and replaced it in 1980, then replaced the 1980 truck in1985 and replaced the 1985 truck in

1989. Every truck was new, so my monthly payments and insurance costs went up each time I bought one.

All during this time, I was trying to get my landscaping business off the ground. It had been my dream since I was a kid. I loved the work. I loved being outdoors. I loved learning about plants. Unfortunately, the business didn't grow because I didn't operate it on a budget. With no budget, I didn't have enough money on hand to pay taxes, pay insurance premiums, buy equipment, etc. I used credit card checks for a lot of that. Big mistakes! I was living in a fantasy world, thinking I had a business that would start to grow, but I was doing nothing to change the situation. I put up with a struggling business, debt, and harassing creditors for years. I hate to have to admit that now, but that is the way it was.

I woke up that May morning in 1989 and wondered if I would ever get out of the miserable mess I had gotten myself into. I am a Christian. I believe God can help in any situation and that He is especially good at helping us in what we think are hopeless situations. I began to pray for His help.

Within days of starting to pray, I came across a man named Larry Burkett while listening to a Christian radio station. Larry was great. He talked about living on a budget and getting out of debt. I felt hope for the first time in a long time. I decided to try making a budget.

My first budget was a mess. After all of my debt payments and the truck payment, I had very little money left over for all of the other areas of the budget. It became clear that I would have to make more money and probably reduce my credit card payments. I should have gotten a second job at that point and contacted my creditors about making lower payments. Instead, I continued trying to grow the landscaping business and just stopped paying some of the creditors.

It wasn't long before the creditors I stopped paying became very aggressive. When you only owe one or two thousand dollars, they don't seem to bother you that much. When you owe fifteen or twenty thousand, they attack you all day every day. They call on the phone, send threatening letters, file law suits, and generally make your life miserable. I experienced first hand the truth in God's Word: "...the borrower is servant to the lender". (Proverbs 22:7 NIV)

I won't try to scare you with all of the unsettling details of how difficult it is to owe money you can't repay. I'll just tell you it is terrible and I don't want you to ever have to go through it.

When the pressure I was feeling was at its strongest, I decided to try making a budget again. This time I prayed even harder for God to help me. Again I came across Larry Burkett on Christian radio. Again he stressed making a budget and living within it. Again my budget showed me that I needed to increase my income and pay my creditors what I could. Even if I couldn't make minimum payments, I should pay them something. It was almost like God was saying, "*Hello*, can you hear me? I'm trying to help you, *again*!"

By now I was willing to do anything. I began looking for a second job to help my budget. I filled out dozens of applications. I never heard back from most of the companies and the ones I did hear back from declined my application. I wondered if my damaged credit was hurting my chances for finding employment. My anxiety about the situation continued.

I prayed and prayed: "Lord, help me out of this mess. I know I'm the one that caused the problem and I have no one to blame but myself, but please, God, I need your help. Lord, I need a second job. Please help me. Amen."

Several days later, I was out submitting applications when I happened to drive by a Sears store in my area of town. There was a portable sign in the parking lot that read "Christmas help wanted". As soon as I saw it, I felt like God was telling me that I should apply for a job there. I pulled into the parking lot and prayed: "Lord, thank you for showing me this sign. I pray that you help me with the application and if this is really your will, clear the way for me so I can start working here. Amen".

I went into the store and filled out an application, just like I had at all the other places I had been, but this time something was different. I felt right at home. God was at work. Two days later I received a call from a lady at the store. She said she wanted me to come in for an interview for part time work in – get this – lawn and garden sales, my specialty. The sign said "Christmas help wanted", but they wanted me for lawn and garden sales. Wow! God was answering my prayers. There is just no other way to explain it.

My first check was fairly small, but it was a great relief to know that Sears had withheld money to pay my taxes. I was also happy that now I had money coming in during the winter time. Those two things made it possible for me to make a budget that would actually work. God was working overtime on my "impossible situation".

During this time I came across an encouraging verse in the book of Ephesians: "Now glory be to God who by His mighty power at work within us is able to do far more than we would even dare to ask or ever dream of – infinitely beyond our highest prayers, desires, thoughts, or hopes". (Ephesians 3:20 TLB)

I had prayed for God to help me out of my financial mess. He heard my prayers and began moving. He brought Larry Burkett's teaching to me. He gave me a second job that was right in line with the other job I had – my landscaping business. He blessed me with winter time income and help in paying my taxes. He blessed me with the strength to follow through with the budget and negotiate with my creditors even though both were difficult at first. God is good! As the song says, "Our God is an Awesome God".

My first several budgets after starting work at Sears were pretty tight. Some of the creditors did reduce my payments, but paying them back was still very slow and very painful.

When spring rolled around, everything God had put in place for me began to grow, and grow rapidly. Sears upgraded my status to full time. Soon I was making fairly good money and had health insurance, dental insurance, life insurance, a 401(k) and a discount on lawn and garden equipment that I could use in my landscaping business.

The longer hours at Sears caused me to make that my main job and the landscaping business my second job. That was fine with me. I would still get to work outdoors two days a week while making steady money with Sears the other days of the week.

After five months working full time at Sears my budget was easier to make. I was able to pay all of my regular bills, pay a little extra on my debts and still save several hundred dollars a month.

As time went by, I was able to increase my debt payments. God was still helping me even when things seemed to be going well. When one of my oldest credit card accounts was sold to another collection agency, they threatened to sue if I did not pay the entire balance within 30 days. I had saved for that possibility, but I didn't have enough money to pay off the account. Miraculously, God provided the rest of the money and I was able to get rid of the debt.

Today, my wife and I are debt free accept for our house. I plan our budget every month and we work hard to stay within its limits. When we fail and overspend, we don't give up; we correct the problem and move ahead once again. Our budget is simple but it is complete. We are able to give, save, pay our taxes on time, pay all of our bills on time, and splurge a little here and there. "Thank you, Lord".

In March of 2007, I began to sense that God was going to lead me in a different direction with my work. What the change would be I didn't know. I prayed and waited. In the spring of 2008, a series of circumstances made it clear that the change was coming and it was coming soon. It came on August 2, 2008 when I resigned my job at Sears.

A few days after I submitted my resignation, though, I had second thoughts. I prayed for God to show me if He really had something new for me or if I had misinterpreted His will and should stay at Sears. Assurance came when I felt God telling me to review my priorities and live my life in the way that He was leading. In my prayer times I became confident that God was telling me that it was okay to leave Sears and that He would show me what He wanted me to do next.

I am thrilled with the new work God has given me. He has placed on my heart a desire to help Christian young people like you avoid the mistakes I have made with money. This book is part of that new work.

In the pages ahead you will learn about what I call the Good Cent$ Budget. I want you to begin using the budget today and continue it for the rest of your life. I also want you to pray for God to help you work out your budget. When God is leading you, you will be blessed. Also, consider this, living without a budget is living in a fantasy world. I know because I lived in that world for a long time. Living on a budget is living in reality. I know because I now live there.

My prayer for you is that you get off to a good start in your financial life and that it never becomes a problem for you. Do what most people don't do – live on a budget.

Review:

How much money did I owe in 1989?

_____

_____

_____

Who did I owe?

_____

_____

_____

_____

What did a collector call me?

_____

_____

_____

_____

How much did I learn about personal finances at home, in school and at church?

_____

_____

_____

_____

Are there any verses in the Bible on finances?

_____

_____

_____

_____

List 4 things the credit card salesman said about the credit card he was trying to push on me.

_____

_____

_____

_____

What was the wrong turn I took?

_____

_____

_____

What does "minimum payment" on a credit card mean?

_____

_____

_____

What was my plan for my two department store credit cards?

_____

_____

_____

What caused that plan to fail?

_____

_____

_____

How did I make my debt situation worse when my plan failed?

_____

_____

_____

What mistake did I make paying taxes and buying equipment in my landscaping business?

_____

_____

_____

_____

What did I do to start turning things around?

_____

_____

_____

How well did I do the first time I tried to make a budget?

_____

_____

_____

Why did my landscaping business struggle?

_____

_____

_____

When the pressure was at its greatest, what did I do?

_____

_____

_____

_____

How did God work in my situation?

_____

_____

_____

_____

I thought all I needed was a second job, what other blessings did God add to what I prayed for?

_____

_____

_____

_____

Even when things were going well, how did God continue to help me?

_____

_____

_____

_____

What is my financial situation today?

_____

_____

_____

_____

What made me decide to leave the job God gave me?

_____

_____

_____

What did God lead me to do after leaving the job He had given me?

_____

_____

_____

What do I want you to start doing today?

_____

_____

_____

Running the Race

Help me, Father,
from start to finish,
to jump the hurdles,
endure fatigue,
uphold my fellow runners,
and persevere
to glorious victory
for Christ. Amen!

Good Cent$ Focus

Start a budget today and live on it the rest of your life.
Living on a budget is living in reality.
Not living on a budget is living in a fantasy world.
Do what most people don't do – Live on a budget

Memorize the Good Cent$ Focus before moving on.

2
GOOD CENT$ OVERVIEW

The remainder of this book is divided into the following chapters:

<u>Chapter 3 - The Good Cent$ Budget:</u>
This chapter gives you the tools you need to work the Good Cent$ Budget. Read the notes about budgeting in general and be sure to memorize the focus of this book before taking a look at the basic framework of the Good Cent$ Budget.

Next, take a look at some Good Cent$ about every section of the budget starting with income and continuing with giving, saving, taxes, housing, transportation, food/household, insurance, debt, below the balance (see note below), miscellaneous and all other expenses.

Following that, there will be a Good Cent$ Instruction Sheet for you to refer to when you begin planning your budget on paper.

After the instruction sheet, you will see several examples of Good Cent$ Budgets from basic to more complex. Those will be followed by an explanation of the all important Results page that shows how well you are doing for the month and how well you are doing for the year.

<u>Chapter 4 - Good Cent$ for Married Couples:</u>
This is a brief, but important section about finances for Married Couples. Read this section whether you are married or not.

Chapter 5 - Good Cent$ from Good People:

Good Cent$ from Good People consists of quotes from Christians I respect very highly. Study the quotes and get every bit of wisdom out of them that you can.

Chapter 6 - Good Cent$ Q & A:

Be sure to read the questions and answers as they may address some of your own questions about budgeting in general and the Good Cent$ Budget in particular.

Chapter 7 - A Good Cent$ Exercise:

You will have a chance to list the benefits and problems associated with budgeting and decide if it's wise to live on a budget for the rest of your life.

Chapter 8 - Final Thoughts:

This section is to encourage you as you start your budget and continue it for the rest of your life. Never give up!

I mentioned at the beginning of this book that most of the information would be presented in "bullet" form. Here are a few bullets to get you ready for the fusillade of bullets to come:

- Read this entire book before you begin planning your budget.
- Re-read Good Cent$ at least once a year.
- Take the information you learn here and use your brain to figure out your budget, your "below the balance" accounts and your spending record. Make the Good Cent$ Budget work for you.
- Our Good Cent$ verse is Proverbs 16:3: "Commit your work to the Lord, then it will succeed." TLB

Note: Below the Balance. You will see several references to this as you read through the rest of the book. Below the balance is simply a means of saving money in a regular checking or savings account. You deposit money into your account but you do not add the funds to the useable balance in your register. Keep a separate register that only records your below the balance deposits. The money you collect below the balance can be divided into various "accounts" to cover emergencies, gifts, vacations, down payment on a car, etc. It is a great way to accumulate money. There will be more about this in the section covering below the balance in the Good Cent$ Budget.

Review:

What should you do before planning your budget?

_____

_____

_____

_____

What is "Below the Balance"?

_____

_____

_____

_____

How often should you re-read this book?

_____

_____

_____

_____

What is the Good Cent$ verse?

_____

_____

_____

_____

3
THE GOOD CENT$ BUDGET

It's time to start learning the Good Cent$ Budget. The "bullets" are about to start flying. Read each point carefully and think about what it would mean to your life. Let's start with some Good Cent$ about budgets.

Good Cent$ about a budget

- Start living on a budget today and continue it for the rest of your life.

- Living on a budget is living in reality.

- Not living on a budget is living in a fantasy world.

- Do what most people don't do – live on a budget.

- A budget is simply a plan for adjusting spending to income. Did you get that? It is a plan for adjusting spending to income. Why would anyone not want to adjust their spending to be within their income? It's crazy!!!!!!!!! Businesses, governments, churches, charitable institutions, etc., all have to operate on a budget, and so do people.

- Living on a budget takes a little work, but it is vitally important to your overall success and happiness in life.

- It is very important that you keep a good attitude about your budget. Don't let the challenges of keeping a budget cause you to give up and miss out on all of the many blessings that come with staying with it.

- With a budget you don't have to spend a lot of time thinking about money. Your budget does all of that for you.

- With a budget you will be able to help other people financially.

- With a budget you will be able to save money.

- With a budget you will be able to pay your taxes on time.

- With a budget you will be able to avoid debt. If you already have debt, you will be able to pay it off and avoid it in the future.

- With a budget you can take debt-free vacations.

- With a budget you can enjoy debt-free Christmases.

- With a budget you won't have to worry about unexpected home or auto repairs.

- With a budget you won't have to fear medical bills or temporary unemployment.

- With a budget you can look forward to your "retirement" years.

- As you go through life and your income and expenses increase, your budget will grow with you.

- If you are like me, you will begin to enjoy budgeting and look forward to making your budget each month. There is a great feeling that comes from successfully getting through a month with a balanced budget. Most people never experience this great feeling because most people don't live on a budget.

- The Good Cent$ Budget is a monthly budget plan. You will write 12 budgets during the year.

- The Good Cent$ Budget does not require a lot of forms or detailed calculations. Each month you will simply create your budget on a sheet of paper based on your estimated income. Once a day you will record your expenses in a notebook. A total of 2 hours a month should get the job done. (There are 720 hours in a 30 day month.) You can either use a cash system with envelopes or a standard checking account to manage cash flow.

- The Good Cent$ Budget is a framework for you to adjust in any way you like. You can add categories or remove them as you see fit and as your budget allows. The important point is for you to start living on a budget today and continue it for the rest of your life.

Review:

When should you start living on a budget?

_____

_____

_____

_____

What is a budget?

_____

_____

_____

_____

What are some of the many blessings that come with keeping a budget?

_____

_____

_____

_____

How often should you write your budget?

_____

_____

_____

_____

How many hours are in a month and how many hours a month does it take to plan and record your budget?

_____

_____

_____

_____

What you will need:

1 Pen
3 Spiral notebooks (Checking register, Spending record and Below balance)
1 Calculator
1 Brain
1 Determination to start the Good Cent$ Budget and continue it for the rest of your life.

Or you can create and maintain your budget on your computer.

Now let's take a quick look at the basic Good Cent$ Budget.

The three categories above the bold line are priorities and should be funded first.

The categories after the bold line are where you will spend your remaining income for the month. You have a lot of flexibility in funding these categories, especially Miscellaneous and All Other. You can add categories at any time.

If all of this seems a little overwhelming to you, just hang on and keep reading.

The Good Cent$ Budget

Estimated income for the month_____

1. GIVING
2. SAVING
3. TAXES
4. HOUSING
5. TRANSPORTATION
6. FOOD/HOUSEHOLD
7. INSURANCE
8. DEBTS
9. BELOW THE BALANCE
10. MISCELANEOUS.
11. ALL OTHER

Review:

What will you need for the Good Cent$ Budget?

_____

_____

_____

_____

What are the first three categories in the good Cent$ Budget?

_____

_____

_____

Now let's look at each category in the Good Cent$ Budget.

Good Cent$ about Income

- The entire budget is built around your income. It is the first category in your budget.

- Making a budget will tell you a lot about your income. Remember in my story, when I made my first budget, it showed me that I needed to make more money.

- Of course, your income will start low in the early days of your working life.

- Your income will rise as you continue on in your working life.

- Hard work and continuing education can increase your income.

- "Whatever you do, work at it with all your heart, as working for the Lord, not for men." (Colossians 3:23 NIV)

- Let your personal education be a lifelong adventure. It is absolutely critical that you graduate from high school or get a GED. It is great if you can attend college and even better if you can graduate. The best of all worlds is to graduate from college or a trade school with a degree or certification in a field you love.

- Read as much as you can during and after your school years. Reading is a lifetime sport.

- Read and study God's Word – The Bible. There is an eternity of knowledge within its pages. There are over 2000 verses that directly or indirectly relate to money.

- Ask a lot of questions.

- Make as much money as you can without letting the pursuit of money harm any other areas of your life.

- Remember our Good Cent$ verse: "Commit to the Lord whatever you do, and your plans will succeed." (Proverbs 16:3 NIV)

- Work hard. Rest. Work hard again. Rest again. Repeat this process all your life.
- I don't like to be negative, but I need to tell you that there are two things that cause a lot of the poverty in this world – Ignorance and laziness. Don't let them steal your income.
- Always thank God for the income He blesses you with.

Review:

What can increase your income?

_____

_____

_____

_____

When can you stop reading?

_____

_____

_____

_____

Does the Bible mention anything about finances?

_____

_____

_____

_____

What two things cause a lot of poverty in the world?

_____

_____

_____

_____

Good Cent$ about Giving

- Pray about how much to give to God. I believe 10% is a great place to start.

- Study God's Word about giving to decide what you should do. Remember, He will give you every cent you will ever have so give some of it back to Him.

- With giving in mind, meditate on the following: "Jesus replied, 'Love the Lord your God with all your heart and with all your soul and with all your mind' …'Love your neighbor as yourself'." (Matthew 22:37-39 NIV)

- You give back to God by giving to your church, to family members in need, to friends in need, and even to strangers God leads you to help. You also give back to God by giving to Christian teachers, missionaries, Christian scholarship funds, etc.

- Give first or you probably won't give at all.

- Giving can be the most rewarding category in your budget.

- "Remember this: Whoever sows sparingly will also reap sparingly, and whoever sows generously will also reap generously. Each man should give what he has decided in his heart to give, not reluctantly or under compulsion, for God loves a cheerful giver." (2 Corinthians 9:6-7 NIV)

- It is wise to keep records of your giving. Some giving is tax deductible.

- It is not wise to talk about your giving. Keep it between you and God.

- "But when you give to the needy, do not let your left hand know what your right hand is doing, so that your giving may be in secret. Then your Father, who sees what is done in secret, will reward you." (Matthew 6:3-4 NIV)

Review:

How do you give back to God?

_____

_____

_____

_____

Should you talk about your giving?

_____

_____

_____

_____

Good Cent$ about Saving

- After giving back to God, saving (for your future and to avoid debt) is the most important category in your budget.

- Save some of your income every month.

- Pray about how much to save.

- After you have prayed – and as you continue to pray – make a list of goals for your saving. List short-term goals (One week to six months), long-term goals (Six months to five years), and life goals (Five years and beyond). Review these goals regularly and revise as needed.

- Saving even small amounts of money over a long period of time can meet all of your needs.

- "The plans of the diligent lead to profit, as surely as haste leads to poverty." (Proverbs 21:5 NIV)

- Very important – Save an emergency fund of $1,500 to be used only for emergencies. When you need to use the money for an emergency, be sure to rebuild the fund as quickly as you can. Keep this money below the balance in your checking account.

- Very important – Save a "living fund" that would cover 4 months of your living expenses. You can keep this money in a savings account. It will be a budget saver as well as a "lifesaver" in the event you temporarily lose your ability to make money.

- Save for special projects like auto replacement, electronics, appliances, vacations, Christmas, large gifts, etc. Keep this money below the balance in your checking or savings account.

- Save for your retirement. Start with a savings account to build the fund while learning about the many ways to invest to meet your retirement goals. There are many Christian financial experts who can help you with investing for retirement. Don't think you are too young to start thinking about retirement. The earlier you start the easier it is to reach your goals by retirement time or even before then. One of the easiest ways to save is in a 401(K) savings plan where you work. Many employers will match a portion of your investment. These plans tend to grow fairly quickly. Contributions to 401(K) plans are tax deferred. You will be taxed when you begin taking money out of the plan during your retirement years when your tax rate would possibly be lower. There are other types of retirement accounts as well, so check with your employer or trusted investment advisor for more information.

• Here is an example of what you can do with a little extra money and a lot of time: If you opened a savings account on your 20th birthday and paid $250 a month at just 3% interest with an annual tax rate of 25%; on your 67th birthday you would have deposited $141,000 into the account, been paid $145,567 in interest and been taxed $36,392, leaving you with a balance of $250,175 in the account. That $250 a month would be a little tough to come up with in the early years, but as your income grew you would get to a point where you wouldn't have any trouble at all making the payment. You couldn't retire on $250,175, but it would be a good start toward building a portfolio to cover your retirement years.

• I roll coins. Any spare change I have laying around I collect until I have enough to roll. Quarters add up very quickly. At the time of this writing I have rolled over $1,000 in coins. That's a lot of quarters, dimes, nickels, and pennies.

• When you get unexpected money, save a portion of it, then put the rest in any part of the budget you would like.

Review:

How much should you save for emergencies?

_____

_____

_____

_____

How much should you save for a short-term living fund?

_____

_____

_____

_____

When should you begin thinking about retirement?

_____

_____

_____

_____

What should you do with unexpected income?

_____

_____

_____

_____

Good Cent$ about Taxes

- "Tell us therefore, what do you think? Is it lawful to pay taxes to Caesar, or not?" But Jesus perceived their wickedness, and said, "Why do you test me, you hypocrites? Show me the tax money." So they brought Him a denarius and He said to them, "Whose image and inscription is this?" They said to him, "Caesar's." And He said to them, "Render therefore to Caesar the things that are Caesar's, and to God the things that are God's." (Matthew 17:19-21 NKJV)

- Always pay all of your taxes.

- Always pay all of your taxes on time.

- Keep a file with accurate records of income, deductible expenses, and a copy of your tax return. Start a new file each year.

- It is wise to resist the urge to grumble and complain about having to pay your taxes. That won't be easy because everyone around you will be grumbling and complaining about having to pay their taxes.

- One of my landscaping customers once said, "Ed, There are two certainties in life: death and taxes." He looked up and thought for a second then added, "Well, there are probably more than two, but those two bother me the most."

Review:

What did Jesus say about paying taxes?

_____

_____

_____

_____

How often should you start a new file for tax records and information?

_____

_____

_____

Good Cent$ about Housing

- Housing will be the biggest expense category for most people.
- In the Good Cent$ Budget housing includes mortgage or rent and all utilities.
- Very, very, very important: Only live in housing you can afford. This will be more of a challenge later in life when you may be able to afford a larger home. It is then that a lot of people "overreach" and go into debt for housing that is beyond their ability to comfortably repay.
- It is wise to have a substantial down payment saved before buying a house. Your down payment should be at least 20%.
- Many people will tell you that it is cheaper to buy a house than to rent one. That is not always true. The monthly payment to own a house may be lower than the monthly payment to rent the same house, but there are a lot more costs involved in home ownership than in renting. Consider the costs that go along with home ownership before you decide to buy.
- Start a below the balance account to save for upgrades to your housing.
- Start a below the balance account to save for home repairs.
- Wait a minute, that customer of mine was right, there are three certainties in life: death, taxes and home repairs.
- Start praying now that God would lead you to the places He wants you to live as you go through this life. If He leads you there, He will bless you with a way to pay for it.

Review:

What is included in the housing category of the Good Cent$ budget?

_____

_____

_____

_____

What is the only kind of housing you should live in?

_____

_____

_____

_____

What can you do to protect your budget from the cost of unexpected home repairs?

_____

_____

_____

_____

Good Cent$ about Transportation

- Very important – only buy a car or truck you can afford.

- Save as much as you can for a car before you go shopping for one.

- It is wise to pay off the balance on a car as soon as you can and then start saving for your next car. When you are ready to shop for your next vehicle you will have a trade-in and a cash down payment. I call this "trade-in and save."

- With trade-in and save, you will be able to get a better, more dependable vehicle every time you purchase one.

- Eventually, you will be able to trade in your old car and pay cash for the balance due on the new one. That will be a great day because you will have even longer to save for your next vehicle.

- Consider insurance costs when buying a car.

- Consider gas mileage when buying a car.

- You may have to buy a real clunker at first, but if you continue to trade-in and save, you will be driving a nice car in a few years.

- Start a below the balance account for auto repairs.

- Hey, there are four certainties in life: death, taxes, home repairs, and auto repairs.

- Don't pay attention to automobile sales hype. Let your budget and your trade-in and save plan show you which vehicle you can afford to own.

- New cars and trucks are so over priced that they lose value as soon as you drive them off the dealer's lot.

- Transportation gets a lot of people into financial trouble. Don't let that happen to you.

- Put your patience on and wear it awhile before making decisions about buying cars and, of course, pray about it.

Review:

What should you do before shopping for a car or truck?

_____

_____

_____

_____

What is the "trade-in and save" plan?

_____

_____

_____

_____

How can you protect your budget from the cost of unexpected auto repairs?

_____

_____

_____

_____

How soon do new cars and trucks begin to lose their value?

_____

_____

_____

_____

Good Cent$ about Food/Household

- This is a sneaky category. You will have to pay close attention to how much money and how much month you have left for food/household.

- Food/household includes groceries, restaurants, and fast food, as well as bath soap, toothpaste, deodorant, cleaning supplies, light bulbs, etc.

- It is wise to over-fund this category when starting your budget. Adjust the food/household budget each month until you get a realistic amount that runs down to zero by the end of the month.

- Once you get a realistic amount for food/household, try to cut it down a bit over time.

- Be sure to plan more for this category during holiday months.

- Your budget can include a built-in diet plan. Budget a little less for food/household and watch the pounds drop off.

Review:

What is included in the food/household category of the Good Cent$ budget?

_____

_____

_____

_____

How much money would you place in this category?

_____

_____

_____

Good Cent$ about Insurance

- The correct amount of insurance is based on your need and ability to pay. As you go through life, both need and ability to pay will change.

- Shop around. Get quotes from several companies before deciding to buy a policy.

- Shop around every time your insurance is about to renew.

- You can lower the cost of an insurance policy by increasing the deductible amount. If you do this, be sure to save the deductible amount below the balance or in a savings account.

- It is wise to be insured. It is unwise to overpay for insurance or to get more or less coverage than you need. Work hard to get the correct amount of coverage at the best possible price.

- If you get married, you should purchase life insurance. If you have kids, you simply must have life insurance. Basically, if you have dependents, you need life insurance.

- Term life insurance plans are generally better values than whole life plans. Research the difference between the two and decide which one is best for you.

- There are insurance sales people out there who will try to get you to look at life insurance as an investment. Don't fall for that. Life insurance is for protecting your dependents if you died. It is not for investing.

Review:

What is the correct amount of insurance?

_____

_____

_____

_____

How can you lower the cost of insurance?

_____

_____

_____

_____

When should you get life insurance?

_____

_____

_____

_____

Should you use life insurance as an investment?

_____

_____

_____

_____

- If you are in debt now, the first thing you must do is STOP GOING FURTHER INTO DEBT. Stop using credit cards or borrowing money.

- If you have debt, work hard to pay it off as quickly as possible.

- Having debt at a young age doesn't mean you are a bad person, but it could mean that you are headed for a difficult life if you continue to pay for things with money you don't have.

- A lot of people in this country have credit card debt. Does that mean it is okay? No, it means that all of those people have a problem – a problem you don't need.

- Make a list of your debts so you will know exactly how much you owe. Just doing this may be all you need to start getting rid of your debt.

- The best way to get rid of debt is to start with the smallest debt first and focus on it all day everyday until you get it paid off. Pay the minimum due on the other accounts. Then go just as hard after the next smallest account and do whatever you have to do to pay it off as quickly as possible while still paying the minimum on all of the other accounts. You may have to get a second job temporarily to get rid of all of your debts.

- Try to make debt payoff fun. Celebrate every victory no matter how small. Have a big "bye-bye debt" party when you finally pay off the last dollar.

- Very important: Credit card debt is financial cancer. It can destroy your financial health.

- Very important: Student loans must be repaid. Decide on a plan for repayment even before you get the loan. Stick to your payoff plan until all of the loans are gone. A lot of young people fail to do this and suffer many years of financial stress because of it. If you have student loan debt now, begin living on a budget that includes paying off the loans. Don't waste your life stressing about it, just make your budget and pay the loans off as quickly as you can. In a lot of cases, people have to get a second job to pay off student loans. I know it's not fun to get a degree, land a great job, then have to work evenings at a grocery store just to pay off a loan; but keep in mind that the situation won't last forever and better days are coming if you will just stay with it until you pay off the loans.

- Cash is cool!!!!!!!!! It is wise to pay cash as often as possible.

- Checks are still a good way to pay if you keep a checking account register. A checking account register is the little book in a checkbook where you list all of your checks, debits, deposits and balances.

- Debit cards work very well if you keep a checking account register. If you are not disciplined enough to keep a checking account register, my advice would be to hold off on using checks or a debit card. Banks charge hefty fees when you overdraw your account.

- We don't want you to ever overdraw an account, but you can guard against an accidental overdraw by signing up for overdraft protection at your bank.

- Credit cards are not cool, not a good way to pay, and don't work very well for most people. Remember, even people who have good credit and use credit cards can still end up paying a lot of their God-given money in interest to banks.

- "…the borrower is servant to the lender." (Proverbs 22:7 NIV)

- It will be hard at times to resist the temptation to go into debt. It is very wise to resist the temptation.

- It can be a struggle to pay off debts you already have, but it is the honorable thing to do. Don't run from your debts – pay them off.

- Remember the quote at the beginning of this book? "Debt is where you tell God you love Him and want to live for Him and let Him lead you through this life – then you go out and spend more money than He has given you."

Review:

How can you know how much you owe?

_____

_____

_____

_____

What is the best way to pay off multiple debts?

_____

_____

_____

_____

When should you make your payoff plan for student loans?

_____

_____

_____

_____

What is still cool?

_____

_____

_____

_____

Why don't credit cards work very well for most people?

_____

_____

_____

_____

What does the Bible say about borrowers?

_____

_____

_____

_____

What is the honorable thing to do with your debt?

_____

_____

_____

_____

What is the quote about debt at the beginning of this book?

_____

_____

_____

_____

Good Cent$ about Below the Balance

- "Below the balance" refers to funds in a checking account that are not added to the balance in the checking register.

- If you have a checking account with $1,000 in it, but $500 is for various savings accounts, your register balance would be $500. The money shown as your balance is available for normal spending within your budget. The money not shown in the balance is not available for spending.

- Using below the balance is a great way to accumulate money. The money is protected from being spent because it does not appear in your checking account register. You can use the below the balance saving method in a regular savings account as well.

- Keep a separate register in a notebook that only shows below the balance money. In the above example, the $500 below the balance money would be broken down into savings accounts for things like emergencies, special projects, retirement, etc.

- This may seem a little difficult to understand, but it really is very simple. You will get the hang of it quickly and when you do, keeping your below the balance ledger will only take a few minutes a month.

Review:

What is below the balance?

_____

_____

_____

_____

Why do you need 2 checking registers to save below the balance?

_____

_____

_____

_____

Does below the balance make sense to you?

_____

_____

_____

_____

Good Cent$ about Misc.

- I don't like saying miscellaneous, and I sure don't like spelling it, so, we will simply call this category – Misc.
- The Misc. category in your budget includes anything not listed so far, but is a regular monthly payment.
- Examples of Misc. expenses include things like storage rent, cable TV, cell phone, newspaper and magazine subscriptions, etc.
- Items listed here are usually wants instead of needs.
- At any time you can make any Misc. expense a completely separate category in your budget. There is no limit on the number of categories you can have in your budget. Keep in mind, though, that this budget is designed to be as simple as possible. Too many different categories can complicate your budget and possibly make you feel smothered by having every dollar budgeted for specific things.

Review:

What is included in the Misc. category of the Good Cent$ Budget?

_____

_____

_____

_____

What type of item is listed in this category?

_____

_____

_____

How many categories can you have in the Good Cent$ Budget?

_____

_____

_____

_____

Good Cent$ about All Other

- All Other is a category for anything not listed so far in your Good Cent$ budget.

- Usually, items entered here are not regular monthly payments.

- If a payment listed here becomes a regular monthly payment, you can either place it in another category of your budget like Misc., or make a new category just for that payment. This could happen with things like clothes, education expenses, gifts, vacations, Christmas, medical deductibles, etc.

- Remember, there is no limit on the number of categories you can have in the Good Cent$ budget. Remember also that this budget is designed to be as simple as possible. The All Other category lets you have some flexibility with how you spend the money you have left over after all of your regular budget categories have been fully funded for the month.

- Be careful to not overspend in this category.

Review:

What is included in the All Other category of the Good Cent$ Budget?

_____

_____

_____

_____

Again, How many categories can you have in the Good Cent$ Budget?

_____

_____

_____

_____

How does the All Other category give you flexibility in how you spend your money?

_____

_____

_____

_____

Good Cent$ Budget Instruction Sheet

This is a little "cheat sheet" that you can refer to when you actually start creating your first budget.

INCOME: Estimate your total income for the month.

1) GIVING: Decide how much money you want to give away for the month.

2) SAVING: Decide how much money you want to save for the month.

3) TAXES Save for any taxes you have to pay out of your own pocket.

4) HOUSING: Include mortgage, rent, and utilities.

5) TRANSPORTATION: Include auto payments and gas.

6) FOOD/HOUSEHOLD: Include groceries, eating out and household items.

7) INSURANCE: Include all insurance due for the month.

8) DEBTS: Debt reduction payments for the month.

9) BELOW BALANCE: Amount to keep below the balance for the month.

10) MISC.: Any regular payments not listed anywhere else in the budget.

11) ALL OTHER: This will be the amount of money you have left over from your estimated income after all above categories have been funded.

Study these sample budgets and notice the differences between them.

The Good Cent$ Budget
Sample Budget #1

ESTIMATED INCOME FOR THE MONTH _____

1. GIVING
2. SAVING
3. TAXES
4. HOUSING
   Rent
5. TRANSPORTATION
   Gasoline
6. FOOD/HOUSEHOLD
7. INSURANCE
8. DEBTS
9. BELOW BALANCE
10. MISC.
    Cell phone
11. ALL OTHER

This is a very simple budget. Imagine this as your budget. Work with it until you feel comfortable with the amount of money in each category. How much income would it take to make this budget work well for you?

The Good Cent$ Budget
Sample Budget #2

ESTIMATED INCOME FOR THE MONTH _____

1. GIVING
2. SAVING
3. TAXES
4. HOUSING
   Mortgage/rent
5. TRANSPORTATION
   Car payment
   Gasoline
6. FOOD/HOUSEHOLD
7. INSURANCE
8. DEBTS
   Master Card
9. BELOW BALANCE
10. MISC.
    Cable
    Cell phone
11. ALL OTHER

This is also a very simple budget, but with a couple of added sub-categories.

Work with this one until you feel comfortable with the amount of money in each category. How much income would it take to make this budget work well? What categories could cause this budget to fail? Why?

The Good Cent$ Budget
Sample Budget #3

ESTIMATED INCOME FOR THE MONTH _____

1. GIVING
2. SAVING
3. TAXES
4. HOUSING
    Mortgage
    Water
    Electric
    Gas
    Phone
5. TRANSPORTATION
    Car payment
    Gasoline
6. FOOD/HOUSEHOLD
7. INSURANCE
8. DEBTS
    MasterCard
    Visa
9. BELOW BALANCE
10. MISC.
    Storage rent
    Cable
    Cell phone
    Newspaper
11. VACATION
12. CHRISTMAS
13. ALL OTHER

This is still simple, but with even more categories and sub-categories. Work with this one until you feel comfortable with the amount of money in each category. How much income would it take to make this budget work well? What categories could cause this budget to fail? What would you do to make this budget easier to keep?

You have learned a lot. Congratulations! Now it is time to start thinking about your own budget. Use the instruction sheet and the sample budgets as your guides. If you get hung-up in a category, refer back to the Good Cent$ page that covers that category.

Good Cent$ Spending Record

- Now that you are working on your budget, you need to be able to track your progress all through the month. You can do this with a spending record.

- Use a spiral notebook, binder or your computer to record all spending for the month.

- On top of the first page, enter the month you are recording.

- On the very first line of the first page write the category GIVING and the budgeted dollar amount for the month. Every time you give money away during the month, list the amount here.

- Skip down several lines in the notebook and enter SAVING and the budgeted dollar amount for the month. Every time you deposit money into savings, list the amount here.

- Skip down several lines and write TAXES and the budgeted dollar amount for the month. If you pay taxes during the month, list them here.

- Skip down several lines in the notebook and write HOUSING and the budgeted dollar amount for the month.

- Continue repeating in this way until you have listed each category in your budget and the dollar amount you will pay for the month. Be sure to leave plenty of space for categories that will have a lot of entries like TRANSPORTATION, FOOD/HOUSEHOLD, MISC., and ALL OTHER.

- On the last page enter INCOME at the top of the page with estimated income for the month. Every time you receive income during the month, list it here.

- Last, but certainly not least, is the RESULTS page. More on that in a minute.

- After each month is completed, cut off the top right corners of the pages used that month so that you can quickly locate the next month without having to thumb through all the pages of the notebook.

- Your spending record would look something like this:

JULY (Through the 24th)

		Payment	Remaining
1) GIVING 150.00			
7/3	Church	50.00	100.00
7/10	Church	50.00	50.00
7/24	Church	50.00	0.00
2) SAVING 200.00			
7/3	Transfer to saving	25.00	175.00
7/10	Transfer to saving	25.00	150.00
7/17	Transfer to saving	25.00	125.00
7/21	Transfer to saving	35.00	90.00
3) TAXES 75.00			
7/10	Tax account	25.00	50.00
7/20	Tax account	25.00	25.00
7/22	Tax account	25.00	0.00
4) HOUSING 300.00			
7/1	Rent payment	300.00	0.00
5) TRANSPORTATION 340.00			
7/3	Gas	31.75	308.25
7/14	Gas	28.50	279.75
7/15	Truck replacement fund	75.00	204.75
7/22	Gas	31.22	173.53
6) FOOD/HOUSEHOLD 325.00			
7/3	Groceries	38.23	286.77
7/8	Groceries	22.67	264.10
7/14	Groceries	26.98	237.12

7/16	Thornton's Restaurant	21.25	215.87
7/17	Groceries	43.33	172.54
7/22	Groceries	30.87	141.67
7/24	The Big Waffle House	18.99	122.68

7) INSURANCE 200.00
| 7/7 | Monthly Insurance payment | 198.74 | 1.26 |

8) DEBTS 100.00
| 7/14 | Master Card | 50.00 | 50.00 |
| 7/24 | Visa | 50.00 | 0.00 |

9) BELOW BALANCE 50.00
| 7/5 | Pay to below balance | 25.00 | 25.00 |
| 7/18 | Pay to below balance | 25.00 | 0.00 |

10) MISC. 200.00
7/2	Storage Rent	75.00	125.00
7/7	Cell phone	75.55	49.45
7/16	Newspaper	22.00	27.45

11) ALL OTHER 335.00
7/2	Gift card	25.00	310.00
7/3	Bookstore	36.77	273.23
7/4	Baseball tickets	56.00	217.23
7/7	Movies	12.00	205.23
7/10	Below balance Christmas fund	15.00	190.23

12) ESTIMATED INCOME 2250.00
| 7/6 | Regular paycheck | 1,128.89 | 1,128.89 |
| 7/20 | Regular paycheck | 1,128.89 | 2,257.78 |

Good Cent$ Results

- The Results page is for you to grade yourself at the end of each month.

- The Results page will come at the end of the Spending record.

- Results will include Income for the month, Expenses for the month, and Balance for the month. See example below.

- In addition to the monthly totals, the Results page will show you how you are doing for the year. See example below.

- It is OK to run a small surplus each month.

- It is never OK to run a deficit during a month.

- Let any surplus build up in your checking account's regular balance. If the surplus gets large enough, move some of the money into your Below the Balance accounts and keep some of the money as "funny money" for you to use any way you like. Look at it as a reward for having made your budget work. You will deserve it.

- Figuring the results page will be the last thing you do with your budget each month.

- Pray all during the month that God will give you the wisdom and the strength to end the month with a balanced budget.

- Results would be #s 13 and 14 on the spending record above and would look like this:

RESULTS

13. INCOME FOR THE MONTH
    EXPENSES FOR THE MONTH
    BALANCE FOR THE MONTH

14. INCOME FOR THE YEAR
    EXPENSES FOR THE YEAR
    BALANCE FOR THE YEAR

When you put your spending record and results together they look like this:

JULY (Complete month)

		Payment	Remaining
1) GIVING 150.00			
7/3	Church	50.00	100.00
7/10	Church	50.00	50.00
7/24	Church	50.00	0.00
2) SAVING 200.00			
7/3	Transfer to saving	25.00	175.00
7/10	Transfer to saving	25.00	150.00
7/17	Transfer to saving	25.00	125.00
7/21	Transfer to saving	35.00	90.00
7/26	Transfer to saving	90.00	0.00
3) TAXES 75.00			
7/10	Tax account	25.00	50.00
7/20	Tax account	25.00	25.00
7/22	Tax account	25.00	0.00
4)HOUSING 300.00			
7/1	Rent payment	300.00	0.00
5) TRANSPORTATION 340.00			
7/3	Gas	31.75	308.25
7/14	Gas	28.50	279.75
7/15	Truck replacement fund	75.00	204.75
7/22	Gas	31.22	173.53
7/23	Truck replacement fund	100.00	73.53
7/28	Gas	31.26	42.27

6) FOOD/HOUSEHOLD 325.00

7/3	Groceries	38.23	286.77
7/8	Groceries	22.67	264.10
7/14	Groceries	26.98	237.12
7/16	Thornton's Restaurant	21.25	215.87
7/17	Groceries	43.33	172.54
7/22	Groceries	30.87	141.67
7/24	The Big Waffle House	18.99	122.68
7/25	Thornton's Restaurant	23.98	98.70
7/27	Groceries	40.67	58.03
7/31	The Big Waffle House	18.99	39.04
7/31	Burger Barn	8.98	30.06
7/31	Groceries	17.22	12.84
7/31	Popcorn	2.25	10.59

7) INSURANCE 200.00

7/7	Monthly Insurance payment	198.74	1.26

8) DEBTS 100.00

7/14	Master Card	50.00	50.00
7/24	Visa	50.00	0.00

9) BELOW BALANCE 50.00

7/5	Pay to below balance	25.00	25.00
7/18	Pay to below balance	25.00	0.00

10) MISC. 200.00

7/2	Storage Rent	75.00	125.00
7/7	Cell phone	75.55	49.45
7/16	Newspaper	22.00	27.45
7/24	Baseball Magazine subscription	24.99	2.46

11) ALL OTHER 335.00

7/2	Gift card	25.00	310.00
7/3	Bookstore	36.77	273.23
7/4	Baseball Tickets	56.00	217.23
7/7	Movies	12.00	205.23
7/10	Below balance Christmas fund	15.00	190.23
7/12	Garden Supplies	47.80	142.43
7/14	Movies	12.00	130.43
7/16	Motor Oil	3.78	126.65
7/18	Ice Cream	7.88	118.77
7/20	Haircut	19.99	98.78
7/22	T-shirts and Socks	36.27	63.51
7/24	Shoe Polish	4.87	57.64
7/26	Postage	12.33	45.31
7/27	Lawn Fertilizer	23.15	22.16
7/27	Car Wash	6.99	15.17
7/28	Parking	5.00	10.17
7/30	Ice Cream	7.88	2.29
7/31	Toll	1.00	1.29

12) ESTIMATED INCOME 2250.00

7/6	Regular paycheck	1,128.89	1,128.89
7/20	Regular paycheck	1,128.89	2,257.78

RESULTS

13) INCOME FOR THE MONTH   2,257.78
    EXPENSES FOR THE MONTH   2,199.91
    BALANCE FOR THE MONTH   + 57.87

14) INCOME FOR THE YEAR   15,795.28
    EXPENSES FOR THE YEAR   15,574.63
    BALANCE FOR THE YEAR   + 220.65

Congratulations! You have learned how to make your budget, make your spending record, and make them balance at the end of the month. Wow! You now know how to avoid the painful financial mistakes I made early in my life.

Well done!

4

GOOD CENT$ FOR MARRIED COUPLES

- Communicate, communicate, and communicate some more! Talk about your finances.

- According to several recent surveys, 70 – 85% of marriages that ended in divorce failed because of financial troubles. My guess is that most of those financial troubles could have been avoided if the couple had developed a budget before they got married.

- Don't keep secrets. Let your spouse know what you are doing financially.

- You don't have to tell each other every time you buy a cup of coffee, but if an important money matter comes up, talk about it.

- Set some financial goals together. Keep each other up-dated on the progress of the goals. Celebrate together when a goal is reached.

- "For this reason a man shall leave his father and mother and be united to his wife, and they will become one flesh." (Genesis 2:24 NIV) This verse is so important to men and women that God had it written again in the New Testament book of Ephesians (5:31). Since married couples are now "one flesh" in

God's eyes, it seems normal and natural that they would want to handle their finances together.

- Be sure to read the next section, Good Cent$ from Good People. It includes some great insights for married couples.

Review:

What does communication about finances mean to married couples?

_____

_____

_____

_____

What three things should married couples do when setting financial goals?

_____

_____

_____

_____

What does God say about married couples in Genesis and Ephesians?

_____

_____

_____

_____

5
GOOD CENT$ FROM GOOD PEOPLE

I asked some people I respect very highly a question in hopes of getting some Good Cent$ from them that I could pass on to you. Wow! Their comments are amazing. I think it would be very wise for you to read and study the comments and get every ounce of wisdom from them that you can. There will be a space following each quote for you to write down what you learned by reading the quote. As you read, think of how you would answer this question:

What is the most important thing you would want Christian young people to know about how they should handle their money?

Tom Kay – Jersey Village Baptist Church in Houston, Texas
"I have some thoughts about finances for young people just getting started as a married couple.

- Young couples add a lot of stress to their marriage when they get into financial trouble.

- Don't use credit cards at all. You will accumulate debt that will take years to pay off. Use cash or a debit card so you will know when you are running out of money.

- Don't have 'his and her' accounts. This will build distrust between you or cause you to lie to each other about finances.

- Both of you should learn to balance your monthly bank statements so you both know exactly what you have in your checking and savings accounts.

- Try your best to tithe with your joint income. Tithing will keep you close to God and bring many financial blessings to your marriage.

- If you have a payroll saving plan, like a 401(K) at work, by all means use it. It is much easier to have money taken out of your paycheck than trying to do it yourself.

- Sock as much away into savings as you can during your working years so you will be able to live in the way you would like when you retire.

- Go to church as often as you can and train your children in the Lord so they will help you when you get older. "

Review:

What did you learn from these comments?

_____

_____

_____

_____

Did you learn anything new from these comments?

_____

_____

_____

_____

LeAnn Luedeker – Financial Director, Jersey Village Baptist Church
    "Start as you intend to go on (I heard this advice regarding raising children).
    It is so much easier to start giving and saving with your very first paycheck.
    You'll never miss the money! Giving and saving will become part of your ongoing financial plan. You will learn early on how to manage with

the money you have left over instead of spending every penny of your paycheck.

Setting priorities at the beginning will make a big difference in your financial future."

Review:

What did you learn from these comments?

_____

_____

_____

_____

Did you learn anything new from these comments?

_____

_____

_____

_____

Kerry Sanders – HP Executive

"I'd say the most important thing about money for young people to consider is to 'make it in the first place'.

There is a different attitude toward money you have earned vs. money you have been given.

I think there is a sense of entitlement in today's middle class youth. The fundamental lessons of hard work that come with 'making your own money' are not taking place.

I also think the fundamental belief in working hard to earn more money is being lost.

It is good to wisely manage the money you already have. However, it is also good to go out and make more money when you need it. There is nothing immoral about increasing your earnings…when needed."

Review:

What did you learn from these comments?

_____

_____

_____

_____

Did you learn anything new from these comments?

_____

_____

_____

_____

John Murrell – Deacon, St. Rose of Lima, Houston, Texas

"Money has gotten a bad rap. Many people talk about what damage having money can do to young people. It seems the problem is not about money, but rather about us and our attitudes toward money.

The money you have is a gift from God along with the many other gifts He provides. But with all the gifts God has given you, you have to make a choice. Will you use money for the building up of the Kingdom or for your own edification? There are no other choices. There is no middle ground.

All sin falls into 3 categories: the lust of the eyes, the lust of the flesh and the pride of life. Your attitude toward money will make the difference in your steering clear of these traps or falling for them "hook, line and dollar bill."

Review:

What did you learn from these comments?

_____

_____

_____

_____

Did you learn anything new from these comments?

_____

_____

_____

_____

Paul Wallick – Deacon, Jersey Village Baptist Church
"Start tithing early. Use credit very sparingly and wisely. Live within a budget. Do not buy on impulse just because you want something or are trying to keep up with others. Pray about each major purchase before you decide to proceed. Start saving early by putting a portion of your paycheck away each payday. When available, take full advantage of employer match 401(K) contributions (it's free money), teacher retirement plans, IRAs, etc."

Review:

What did you learn from these comments?

_____

_____

_____

_____

Did you learn anything new from these comments?

_____

_____

_____

_____

Anita Wallick – Jersey Village Baptist Church
"Know what God's Word says about money and then do it."

Review:

What did you learn from this comment?

_____

_____

_____

_____

What are some things God's Word says about money?

_____

_____

_____

_____

Ed Hogan – Pastor, Jersey Village Baptist Church

"When I do premarital counseling, we do a whole session on finances. They see it as a huge waste of time. They just assume that all of their financial stuff will work out. They don't talk about finances or make any kind of financial plan; they just fumble around in the darkness. I tell them however they choose to do this…whether he pays the bills or she does… whether they use cash only or debit cards…it must be a team effort. This needs to be agreed to before the marriage – not afterward."

Review:

What did you learn from these comments?

_____

_____

_____

_____

Did you learn anything new from these comments?

_____

_____

_____

_____

Charles Murrell – League City, Texas, father of 3 grown sons.

"The most important action in managing material resources in a life well-lived is appreciating our role as stewards. All we have is consigned to us for only a time and to use according to the Owner's will. This may also be the greatest challenge we face in our valuing of material things.

To fill this role requires first our acceptance of the gift of faith. An individual must choose to believe in having been created just as are the material resources we steward. Peace in dealing with material affairs requires recognition of the true ownership of created things.

For couples, this stewardship must be lived as one. Openness and selfless commitment to sound plans for managing material affairs of the couple form the foundation for happily dealing with the good times and the hard times that inevitably occur. These, after all, are essential elements of the love necessary for a delight-filled life together.

Those principles also apply to individuals and to groups who share material responsibilities. In each case, patient trust that the Source of all good things will provide for us, eases the burden we perceive.

Strength to fulfill this stewardship role is found in close communication with the Owner. This communication of prayer is the most important task for success in our current stewardship role and our preparation for life beyond this material creation."

Review:

What did you learn from these comments?

_____

_____

_____

_____

What did you learn about finances in marriage?

_____

_____

_____

_____

Jeff Moran – Executive Pastor, Jersey Village Baptist Church

"My advice for money management is twofold: save for the future and give in the present. The earlier you begin to give back to God, the more disciplined you will be with your giving later in life. Remember, you cannot out give God.

Stay away from credit card debt and the promise of 'no payment until'. You will have to pay your debts someday and delaying that day is not a solution."

Review:

What did you learn from these comments?

_____

_____

_____

_____

Did you learn anything new from these comments?

_____

_____

_____

_____

Chris Curran – Pastor of Discipleship, Jersey Village Baptist Church

"Practice the spiritual discipline of giving. If you begin to give back to God when you are young, you will find joy in it when you are old. There is no better way to be reminded that all that you have is given to you by God. Knowing that you have invested your money in eternal investments brings true joy.

Do not go into debt. If at all possible, do not carry credit card debt. There may be times when debt is unavoidable (a student loan, car loan, home loan), but if you can learn the habit of not going into debt when you are young, you will be amazed at how much discretionary income you will have.

Live below your means. Even if that means saving just $25.00 each paycheck, you will have money for an emergency and you will be amazed at how much stress that will relieve from your life."

Review:

What did you learn from these comments?

_____

_____

_____

_____

Did you learn anything new from these comments?

_____

_____

_____

_____

Keith Hamilton – Associate Minister of Music, Jersey Village Baptist Church

"The best advice I can give to 15-25 year olds is to save and not spend all their money before they get married and have kids. Resist the urge to spend all you make. If and when you get married and have kids, that savings will come in handy, especially if one of you stays home with the kids."

Review:

What did you learn from these comments?

_____

_____

_____

_____

Did you learn anything new from these comments?

_____

_____

_____

_____

Gregg Matte – Pastor, Houston's First Baptist Church

"The best way to handle money instead of it handling you is to get the flow and order right. The right flow is making sure the outflow is less than the inflow and the right order is to give, save, spend."

Review:

What did you learn from these comments?

_____

_____

_____

_____

Did you learn anything new from these comments?

_____

_____

_____

_____

Kirby Follis – Pastor of Worship, Jersey Village Baptist Church

"My answer would probably be broader than just money and it would apply to me at my age as well as anyone.

One of the main keys to successful money handling is contentment. Many of us want things we can't afford. We engage in unwise spending to get those things. To take it one step further, many times we believe we are entitled to those things and that poor line of thought helps us rationalize an even poorer use of money or credit. Learning to be content with what we have and where we are, instead of comparing ourselves with others, is a great aid in managing money wisely."

Review:

What did you learn from these comments?

_____

_____

_____

_____

Did you learn anything new from these comments?

_____

_____

_____

_____

Randy Murrell – Houston, Texas

"Live within your means. It is easy and can be fun to dream of things that might be a little (or a lot) out of our range of practical affordability, but beware of biting off more than you can chew. Sales and marketing professionals are tasked with making us believe we must have everything they are trying to sell.

Just because a company has a very appealing marketing campaign on a product or service does not mean we have to have it. It can prove to be very uncomfortable and even life changing, to overextend one's financial resources.

Too much unnecessary debt – especially high interest rate credit card debt – can negatively affect one's life for years. Debt seldom results in happiness.

Invest in yourself. As a young adult you have a lot of working years ahead of you. It is important, if you can, to seek out the skills and/or education to do what you want to do. Once you get that education or acquire those skills, continue investing in yourself. Remain an active learner and you will stand out. Your reward for investing in yourself will be waking up each day getting to do what you like to do.

Establish a rainy day fund. Each of us encounters unexpected bumps in the road. Whether it is an auto repair, a medical bill, or a job loss, we can all count on something unexpected happening. Set aside an emergency cash stash.

Take responsibility for your future financial well-being. Waiting on a winning lottery ticket, a big inheritance, or a government handout is not a good way to financial security. Program yourself to be diligent and disciplined in saving and investing. Remember, the earlier you start, the more time you have for your investments to grow. Saving and investing early, systematically, and wisely will also reduce the urge to 'swing for the fences' with your investments later in life.

Review:

What did you learn from these comments?

_____

_____

_____

_____

Did you learn anything new from these comments?

_____

_____

_____

_____

Chan Washington – Deacon, Jersey village Baptist Church

"I urge you to consider my advice as a 62 year old man who worked over 30 years before discovering that God truly cares about how we handle our money and has actually provided many financial guidelines for us in the Bible.

Realize that God owns everything and is your ultimate provider who may choose to work through your human bosses to provide for your needs and direct your path.

Pray specifically for guidance in your career choices and seek to find joy and purpose in each area of your work.

Resolve to allocate every dollar you earn on a 10-10-80 basis.

- 10% - give to the Lord's work.
- 10% - save for yourself
- 80% - spend based on a conservative monthly budget.

Strive to fight off the marketing sales pitches and learn to be content as Paul said in Philippians 4:11-13 "…for I have learned to be content whatever the circumstances. I know what it is to be in need, and I know what it is to have plenty. I have learned the secret of being content in any and every situation, whether well fed or hungry, whether living in plenty or in want. I can do everything through Him who gives me strength." (NIV)

Last year I paid off the final balance on 18 years of college debt for three sons.

This year I will pay off my home and become debt free.

Don't wait as long as I did, but trust the lord and start early in avoiding debt, giving and saving. You can change your family heritage by starting now."

Review:

What did you learn from these comments?

_____

_____

_____

_____

Did you learn anything new from these comments?

_____

_____

_____

_____

The Writer of the Book of Hebrews

"Keep your lives free from the love of money and be content with what you have, because God has said, "Never will I leave you, never will I forsake you." (Hebrews 13:5 NIV)

Review:

What did you learn from this quote?

_____

_____

_____

_____

Did you learn anything new from this quote?

_____

_____

_____

_____

Did you notice any themes running through all of the comments?

_____

_____

_____

_____

What will you do with what you have learned from these comments?

_____

_____

_____

_____

What is the most important thing you would want Christian young people to know about how they should handle their finances?

_____

_____

_____

_____

Will you start living on a budget today?

_____

_____

_____

_____

Will you continue your budget for the rest of your life?

_____

_____

_____

_____

6
GOOD CENT$ Q&A

Can I keep my budget on my computer?

Absolutely! You don't have to use pen and paper. You can figure and maintain your budget in any way you like. If you keep your budget on your computer, be sure to back up your files so you don't lose everything if your computer crashes.

How long will it take for me to know how much money should go into each category?

Most people don't get the numbers right the first time. I know it is disappointing when you work hard to create your first budget, then after a couple of weeks, realize that it is not going to balance at the end of the month. Don't let that discourage you. Like I said in my story, it was difficult making my first few budgets, but I stayed with it and it became easier each month. For me it took about 5 months to get the numbers close to what they needed to be. Some people figure it out in 3 months and some people struggle a bit for the first year. Analyzing your spending record at the end of each month will help you make adjustments that will eventually lead you to the budget that is best for you. Keep at it month by month and you will figure it out.

What about clothes, healthcare, education and things like haircuts? I don't see them in this budget.

You can add any category you like. I will leave that to you. I buy clothes and pay for haircuts with money from the All Other account. I save for healthcare costs in a Below the Balance account. Since my continuing education right now consists mostly of reading, I pay for books, magazines, newspaper etc. with money from the All Other account. The Good Cent$ budget is designed to be as simple as possible and to give you the most flexibility possible in controlling your finances. Use your brain to figure a budget that is best for you.

Once I start making a lot of money, why would I have to continue with this budget thing?

So you can get the most out of the money you worked so hard to get. Without a written budget and an accurately maintained spending record, you will waste a lot of money.

I am getting married soon and we will have two incomes. We will be bringing home way more money than we will need. Do we still need a budget?

Yes! See answer above and consider the need to save for a house, having kids, paying for their education and health care costs, etc. Also, see answer below!

Will I ever get my finances in order and no longer need a budget?

You will get your finances in order, but there will never be a time when you don't need a budget.

Can't I do this in my head?

No. I know you think you can, but it won't work. Without a written budget and an accurately maintained spending record, you will waste a lot of money.

Can I make my budget for each pay period instead of each month?

In all honesty, yes you can. I want you to live on a budget. If the only way you will do that is to budget for each pay period then knock yourself out. Just remember that our financial system operates on a monthly, quarterly and yearly basis. It's just much easier and frankly makes a lot more sense to figure your budget for each month.

What do I do if I don't spend all the money budgeted in a category?

Celebrate! Then check to see if you have over-spent in any other category and if so, apply the money to make that category balance. If you are okay everywhere else in your budget then do whatever you want with the money. You could carry it over into the new month in that category, give it away, put it in your savings account, put it in some of your below the balance accounts or just write yourself a check and have a good time with it.

Do I ever get to have fun on this budget?

Yes you do. You can use money from your All Other account or you can create a separate category for recreation. A budget will not work if you can't have a little fun and recreation in your life. Budget for fun and enjoy.

Can't I just use percentages for each category instead of trying to figure out a dollar amount?

Where's the creativity in that? Sorry, just kidding. If that will work for you, go for it. I still think that as you track your spending you will determine a better number for each category than if you rely on a set percentage.

I don't like the word Budget. Can't you call it something else?

Sorry! No, I can't call it something else. Taking control of your finances is all about personal discipline. Personal discipline takes work and is not always as easy as you might like it to be. Changing the name won't make any of this any easier. Meet it head on and don't let a little six letter word scare you away from taking control of your finances.

Is it Okay to have just one credit card?

No, it's not okay. You don't need it. Use a debit card. Don't be afraid of cash. I'm not saying carry $200 in your wallet or purse, but plan your purchases and have enough cash to do what you want to do. Remember, cash is cool!!!!

Do you recommend online banking?

Yes! You can do almost all banking online these days. I don't get paper statements anymore. All of my statements are sent to me by email each month. You can track your checking account online everyday or even several times a day. Recently I had to replace my debit card due to wear and tear. I called Katherine at my bank and she took care of it for me by ordering a new card that will be sent to my home. You can transfer money between accounts online and you can pay many of your bills online.

Do you recommend Direct Deposit?

Yes! You don't have to worry about losing a paper check. You don't have to stand in line inside a bank or burn gas waiting in line at the drive through window.

And, in most cases, you get paid earlier in the day with Direct Deposit.

In your story you said you liked the teaching of Larry Burkett. Do you recommend any other Christian financial advisors?

Yes. I highly recommend Dave Ramsey and Ron Blue. I also recommend Crown Financial Ministries, the financial teaching of Focus on the Family, and a great little book by Kerby Anderson called "Making the Most of Your Money in Tough times". It would be very wise for you to go to their websites, read their books, listen to them on the radio, etc. and learn all that you can from them.

You said there are over 2,000 verses in the Bible that relate to money. Why didn't you list all of them in this book?

Are you kidding me? Sorry, just joking again. Actually, I want you to find the verses yourself as you read through the Bible. Get a green highlighter and whenever you read your Bible, highlight any verse you find that relates to money or finances. You may find more than 2,000. Since you brought it up, how about listing some verses about money in the space below? If you have a Concordance in the back of your Bible, go there and look for words like money, debt, give, giving, and any other words you think could relate to finances. Refer back to this list often and let God's Word lead you in your personal finances.

Start with our Good Cent$ verse: "Commit your works to the Lord, and your thoughts will be established." (Proverbs 16:3 NKJV)

Bible verses that refer to money:

_____
_____
_____
_____
_____
_____
_____
_____
_____
_____
_____
_____
_____
_____
_____
_____
_____
_____
_____
_____
_____
_____
_____
_____
_____
_____
_____

7
A Good Cent$ Exercise

- Now that you have read most of this book, list the benefits of living on a budget.

- Next, list all of the problems associated with living on a budget.

- Now, analyze your two lists and honestly answer this question: Is it wise to live on a budget for the rest of your life?

Benefits:

_____

_____

_____

_____

_____

Problems:

_____

_____

_____

_____

_____

8
FINAL THOUGHTS

- Pray about your budget. Ask God to help you. When He gives you answers, act on them. As I told you in my story, I didn't follow through on God's answers to my prayers the first time. You don't want God to say, "*Hello*! Can you hear me? I am trying to help you, *again*."

- Open your Bible and keep looking for verses that deal with money. Pray to God using the verses He gives you.

- Never give up on keeping your budget. It may take several months for you to get the numbers right, but you will get them right.

- No matter what your financial situation is right now, start a budget today and continue it for the rest of your life.

- When your budget looks impossible – press on! Keep at it month by month.

- Resist the temptation to give up. Press on!

- Be flexible. As your situation in life changes, your budget will have to change as well. When that happens, you may again be tempted to give up on keeping your budget – don't do it. Figure it out. Get mad at it if you have to, but don't give up. Press on!

- Think about that quote at the beginning of this book: "If you want to be excellent at something, live on a budget. By living on a budget you will be excellent in your personal finances. No matter how average you think you are at everything else, you can be excellent in your personal finances by simply living on a budget."

- Again, don't forget to pray about your budget.

- Remember, living on a budget is living in reality. Not living on a budget is living in a fantasy world.

- In the area of personal finances, do the wise thing, live on a budget.

- Whenever you work on your budget, use Good Cent$.

- Thanks for reading and God bless you as you start your budget and continue it for the rest of your life.

NEVER GIVE UP

Never give up
A simple message to know
Keep walking and praying
A little farther you'll go

Focus is the key
Set your sights on the Lord
Look only at Him
When the pathway is hard

Nothing can break you
The Word is quite clear
It's all happened before
And the Lord is still here

So, press on in your trials
Believe what is true
That God on His Throne
Is taking good care of you

I thank the Lord Jesus Christ for hearing my prayers about my finances and blessing me far beyond what I could have ever hoped or dreamed with His answers. To Him be all the glory, now and forever. Amen.

* [George Sweeting, "Who Said That?" (Chicago; Moody Press, 1995) 330]

** [George Sweeting, "Who Said That?" (Chicago; Moody Press, 1995) 331]

MY GOOD CENT$ BUDGET FOR THE MONTH OF

_____

ESTIMATED INCOME FOR THE MONTH _____

1) GIVING _____

2) SAVING _____

3) TAXES _____

4) HOUSING _____

   Mortgage/Rent _____

   Water _____

   Electric _____

   Gas _____

   Phone _____

5) TRANSPORTATION _____

   Car payment _____

   Gasoline _____

6) FOOD/HOUSEHOLD _____

7) INSURANCE _____

8) DEBTS _____

9) BELOW BALANCE _____

10) MISC. _____

   Cable _____

   Cell Phone _____

   Subscriptions _____

11) VACATION _____

12) CHRISTMAS _____

13) _____

14) _____

15) ALL OTHER _____

MY GOOD CENT$ BUDGET FOR THE MONTH OF

_____

ESTIMATED INCOME FOR THE MONTH _____

1) GIVING _____

2) SAVING _____

3) TAXES _____

4) HOUSING _____

    Mortgage/Rent _____

    Water _____

    Electric _____

    Gas _____

    Phone _____

5) TRANSPORTATION _____

    Car payment _____

    Gasoline _____

6) FOOD/HOUSEHOLD _____

7) INSURANCE _____

8) DEBTS _____

9) BELOW BALANCE _____

10) MISC. _____

    Cable _____

    Cell Phone _____

    Subscriptions _____

11) VACATION _____

12) CHRISTMAS _____

13) _____

14) _____

15) ALL OTHER _____

MY GOOD CENT$ BUDGET FOR THE MONTH OF

_____

ESTIMATED INCOME FOR THE MONTH _____

    1) GIVING   _____

    2) SAVING   _____

    3) TAXES   _____

    4) HOUSING   _____

        Mortgage/Rent   _____

        Water   _____

        Electric   _____

        Gas   _____

        Phone   _____

    5) TRANSPORTATION _____

        Car payment   _____

        Gasoline   _____

    6) FOOD/HOUSEHOLD _____

    7) INSURANCE   _____

    8) DEBTS   _____

    9) BELOW BALANCE   _____

    10) MISC.   _____

        Cable   _____

        Cell Phone   _____

        Subscriptions   _____

    11) VACATION   _____

    12) CHRISTMAS   _____

    13)   _____

    14)   _____

    15) ALL OTHER   _____

MY GOOD CENT$ BUDGET FOR THE MONTH OF

————————————————

ESTIMATED INCOME FOR THE MONTH _____

   1) GIVING   _____

   2) SAVING   _____

   3) TAXES   _____

   4) HOUSING   _____

       Mortgage/Rent   _____

       Water   _____

       Electric   _____

       Gas   _____

       Phone   _____

   5) TRANSPORTATION _____

       Car payment   _____

       Gasoline   _____

   6) FOOD/HOUSEHOLD _____

   7) INSURANCE   _____

   8) DEBTS   _____

   9) BELOW BALANCE   _____

   10) MISC.   _____

       Cable   _____

       Cell Phone   _____

       Subscriptions   _____

   11) VACATION   _____

   12) CHRISTMAS   _____

   13)   _____

   14)   _____

   15) ALL OTHER   _____

MY GOOD CENT$ BUDGET FOR THE MONTH OF

———————————————————

ESTIMATED INCOME FOR THE MONTH _____

    1) GIVING   _____
    2) SAVING   _____
    3) TAXES   _____
    4) HOUSING   _____
        Mortgage/Rent   _____
        Water   _____
        Electric   _____
        Gas   _____
        Phone   _____
    5) TRANSPORTATION   _____
        Car payment   _____
        Gasoline   _____
    6) FOOD/HOUSEHOLD   _____
    7) INSURANCE   _____
    8) DEBTS   _____
    9) BELOW BALANCE   _____
    10) MISC.   _____
        Cable   _____
        Cell Phone   _____
        Subscriptions   _____
    11) VACATION   _____
    12) CHRISTMAS   _____
    13)   _____
    14)   _____
    15) ALL OTHER   _____

MY GOOD CENT$ BUDGET FOR THE MONTH OF

_____

ESTIMATED INCOME FOR THE MONTH _____

1) GIVING   _____

2) SAVING   _____

3) TAXES   _____

4) HOUSING   _____

   Mortgage/Rent   _____

   Water   _____

   Electric   _____

   Gas   _____

   Phone   _____

5) TRANSPORTATION _____

   Car payment   _____

   Gasoline   _____

6) FOOD/HOUSEHOLD _____

7) INSURANCE   _____

8) DEBTS   _____

9) BELOW BALANCE   _____

10) MISC.   _____

   Cable   _____

   Cell Phone   _____

   Subscriptions   _____

11) VACATION   _____

12) CHRISTMAS   _____

13)   _____

14)   _____

15) ALL OTHER   _____

MY GOOD CENT$ BUDGET FOR THE MONTH OF

_____

ESTIMATED INCOME FOR THE MONTH _____

1) GIVING   _____

2) SAVING   _____

3) TAXES   _____

4) HOUSING   _____

   Mortgage/Rent   _____

   Water   _____

   Electric   _____

   Gas   _____

   Phone   _____

5) TRANSPORTATION   _____

   Car payment   _____

   Gasoline   _____

6) FOOD/HOUSEHOLD   _____

7) INSURANCE   _____

8) DEBTS   _____

9) BELOW BALANCE   _____

10) MISC.   _____

   Cable   _____

   Cell Phone   _____

   Subscriptions   _____

11) VACATION   _____

12) CHRISTMAS   _____

13)   _____

14)   _____

15) ALL OTHER   _____

MY GOOD CENT$ BUDGET FOR THE MONTH OF

_____

ESTIMATED INCOME FOR THE MONTH _____

1) GIVING   _____

2) SAVING   _____

3) TAXES   _____

4) HOUSING   _____

    Mortgage/Rent   _____

    Water   _____

    Electric   _____

    Gas   _____

    Phone   _____

5) TRANSPORTATION   _____

    Car payment   _____

    Gasoline   _____

6) FOOD/HOUSEHOLD   _____

7) INSURANCE   _____

8) DEBTS   _____

9) BELOW BALANCE   _____

10) MISC.   _____

    Cable   _____

    Cell Phone   _____

    Subscriptions   _____

11) VACATION   _____

12) CHRISTMAS   _____

13)   _____

14)   _____

15) ALL OTHER   _____

MY GOOD CENT$ BUDGET FOR THE MONTH OF

_____

ESTIMATED INCOME FOR THE MONTH _____

1) GIVING   _____

2) SAVING   _____

3) TAXES   _____

4) HOUSING   _____

    Mortgage/Rent   _____

    Water   _____

    Electric   _____

    Gas   _____

    Phone   _____

5) TRANSPORTATION   _____

    Car payment   _____

    Gasoline   _____

6) FOOD/HOUSEHOLD   _____

7) INSURANCE   _____

8) DEBTS   _____

9) BELOW BALANCE   _____

10) MISC.   _____

    Cable   _____

    Cell Phone   _____

    Subscriptions   _____

11) VACATION   _____

12) CHRISTMAS   _____

13)   _____

14)   _____

15) ALL OTHER   _____

MY GOOD CENT$ BUDGET FOR THE MONTH OF

––––––––––––––––––––––––––

ESTIMATED INCOME FOR THE MONTH _____

    1) GIVING   _____

    2) SAVING   _____

    3) TAXES   _____

    4) HOUSING   _____

        Mortgage/Rent   _____

        Water   _____

        Electric   _____

        Gas   _____

        Phone   _____

    5) TRANSPORTATION _____

        Car payment   _____

        Gasoline   _____

    6) FOOD/HOUSEHOLD _____

    7) INSURANCE   _____

    8) DEBTS   _____

    9) BELOW BALANCE   _____

    10) MISC.   _____

        Cable   _____

        Cell Phone   _____

        Subscriptions   _____

    11) VACATION   _____

    12) CHRISTMAS   _____

    13)   _____

    14)   _____

    15) ALL OTHER   _____

MY GOOD CENT$ BUDGET FOR THE MONTH OF

_____

ESTIMATED INCOME FOR THE MONTH _____

   1) GIVING   _____

   2) SAVING   _____

   3) TAXES   _____

   4) HOUSING   _____

      Mortgage/Rent   _____

      Water   _____

      Electric   _____

      Gas   _____

      Phone   _____

   5) TRANSPORTATION _____

      Car payment   _____

      Gasoline   _____

   6) FOOD/HOUSEHOLD _____

   7) INSURANCE   _____

   8) DEBTS   _____

   9) BELOW BALANCE   _____

   10) MISC.   _____

      Cable   _____

      Cell Phone   _____

      Subscriptions   _____

   11) VACATION   _____

   12) CHRISTMAS   _____

   13)   _____

   14)   _____

   15) ALL OTHER   _____

MY GOOD CENT$ BUDGET FOR THE MONTH OF

_____

ESTIMATED INCOME FOR THE MONTH _____

- 1) GIVING _____
- 2) SAVING _____
- 3) TAXES _____
- 4) HOUSING _____
  - Mortgage/Rent _____
  - Water _____
  - Electric _____
  - Gas _____
  - Phone _____
- 5) TRANSPORTATION _____
  - Car payment _____
  - Gasoline _____
- 6) FOOD/HOUSEHOLD _____
- 7) INSURANCE _____
- 8) DEBTS _____
- 9) BELOW BALANCE _____
- 10) MISC. _____
  - Cable _____
  - Cell Phone _____
  - Subscriptions _____
- 11) VACATION _____
- 12) CHRISTMAS _____
- 13) _____
- 14) _____
- 15) ALL OTHER _____

MY GOOD CENT$ BUDGET FOR THE MONTH OF

_____

ESTIMATED INCOME FOR THE MONTH _____

1) GIVING _____

2) SAVING _____

3) TAXES _____

4) HOUSING _____

   Mortgage/Rent _____

   Water _____

   Electric _____

   Gas _____

   Phone _____

5) TRANSPORTATION _____

   Car payment _____

   Gasoline _____

6) FOOD/HOUSEHOLD _____

7) INSURANCE _____

8) DEBTS _____

9) BELOW BALANCE _____

10) MISC. _____

   Cable _____

   Cell Phone _____

   Subscriptions _____

11) VACATION _____

12) CHRISTMAS _____

13) _____

14) _____

15) ALL OTHER _____

MY GOOD CENT$ BUDGET FOR THE MONTH OF

————————————————————

ESTIMATED INCOME FOR THE MONTH _____

    1) GIVING   _____

    2) SAVING   _____

    3) TAXES   _____

    4) HOUSING   _____

       Mortgage/Rent   _____

       Water   _____

       Electric   _____

       Gas   _____

       Phone   _____

    5) TRANSPORTATION _____

       Car payment   _____

       Gasoline   _____

    6) FOOD/HOUSEHOLD _____

    7) INSURANCE   _____

    8) DEBTS   _____

    9) BELOW BALANCE   _____

    10) MISC.   _____

       Cable   _____

       Cell Phone   _____

       Subscriptions   _____

    11) VACATION   _____

    12) CHRISTMAS   _____

    13)   _____

    14)   _____

    15) ALL OTHER   _____

MY GOOD CENT$ BUDGET FOR THE MONTH OF

_____

ESTIMATED INCOME FOR THE MONTH _____

1) GIVING   _____

2) SAVING   _____

3) TAXES   _____

4) HOUSING   _____

    Mortgage/Rent   _____

    Water   _____

    Electric   _____

    Gas   _____

    Phone   _____

5) TRANSPORTATION _____

    Car payment   _____

    Gasoline   _____

6) FOOD/HOUSEHOLD _____

7) INSURANCE   _____

8) DEBTS   _____

9) BELOW BALANCE   _____

10) MISC.   _____

    Cable   _____

    Cell Phone   _____

    Subscriptions   _____

11) VACATION   _____

12) CHRISTMAS   _____

13)   _____

14)   _____

15) ALL OTHER   _____

MY GOOD CENT$ BUDGET FOR THE MONTH OF

_____

ESTIMATED INCOME FOR THE MONTH _____

1) GIVING   _____

2) SAVING   _____

3) TAXES   _____

4) HOUSING   _____

     Mortgage/Rent   _____

     Water   _____

     Electric   _____

     Gas   _____

     Phone   _____

5) TRANSPORTATION   _____

     Car payment   _____

     Gasoline   _____

6) FOOD/HOUSEHOLD   _____

7) INSURANCE   _____

8) DEBTS   _____

9) BELOW BALANCE   _____

10) MISC.   _____

     Cable   _____

     Cell Phone   _____

     Subscriptions   _____

11) VACATION   _____

12) CHRISTMAS   _____

13)   _____

14)   _____

15) ALL OTHER   _____

MY GOOD CENT$ BUDGET FOR THE MONTH OF

_____

ESTIMATED INCOME FOR THE MONTH _____

    1) GIVING   _____

    2) SAVING   _____

    3) TAXES   _____

    4) HOUSING   _____

        Mortgage/Rent   _____

        Water   _____

        Electric   _____

        Gas   _____

        Phone   _____

    5) TRANSPORTATION   _____

        Car payment   _____

        Gasoline   _____

    6) FOOD/HOUSEHOLD   _____

    7) INSURANCE   _____

    8) DEBTS   _____

    9) BELOW BALANCE   _____

    10) MISC.   _____

        Cable   _____

        Cell Phone   _____

        Subscriptions   _____

    11) VACATION   _____

    12) CHRISTMAS   _____

    13)   _____

    14)   _____

    15) ALL OTHER   _____

MY GOOD CENT$ BUDGET FOR THE MONTH OF

_____

ESTIMATED INCOME FOR THE MONTH _____

- 1) GIVING   _____
- 2) SAVING   _____
- 3) TAXES   _____
- 4) HOUSING   _____
  - Mortgage/Rent   _____
  - Water   _____
  - Electric   _____
  - Gas   _____
  - Phone   _____
- 5) TRANSPORTATION _____
  - Car payment   _____
  - Gasoline   _____
- 6) FOOD/HOUSEHOLD _____
- 7) INSURANCE   _____
- 8) DEBTS   _____
- 9) BELOW BALANCE   _____
- 10) MISC.   _____
  - Cable   _____
  - Cell Phone   _____
  - Subscriptions   _____
- 11) VACATION   _____
- 12) CHRISTMAS   _____
- 13)   _____
- 14)   _____
- 15) ALL OTHER   _____

MY GOOD CENT$ BUDGET FOR THE MONTH OF

_____

ESTIMATED INCOME FOR THE MONTH _____

    1) GIVING _____

    2) SAVING _____

    3) TAXES _____

    4) HOUSING _____

        Mortgage/Rent _____

        Water _____

        Electric _____

        Gas _____

        Phone _____

    5) TRANSPORTATION _____

        Car payment _____

        Gasoline _____

    6) FOOD/HOUSEHOLD _____

    7) INSURANCE _____

    8) DEBTS _____

    9) BELOW BALANCE _____

    10) MISC. _____

        Cable _____

        Cell Phone _____

        Subscriptions _____

    11) VACATION _____

    12) CHRISTMAS _____

    13) _____

    14) _____

    15) ALL OTHER _____

MY GOOD CENT$ BUDGET FOR THE MONTH OF

_____

ESTIMATED INCOME FOR THE MONTH _____

- 1) GIVING _____
- 2) SAVING _____
- 3) TAXES _____
- 4) HOUSING _____
  - Mortgage/Rent _____
  - Water _____
  - Electric _____
  - Gas _____
  - Phone _____
- 5) TRANSPORTATION _____
  - Car payment _____
  - Gasoline _____
- 6) FOOD/HOUSEHOLD _____
- 7) INSURANCE _____
- 8) DEBTS _____
- 9) BELOW BALANCE _____
- 10) MISC. _____
  - Cable _____
  - Cell Phone _____
  - Subscriptions _____
- 11) VACATION _____
- 12) CHRISTMAS _____
- 13) _____
- 14) _____
- 15) ALL OTHER _____

MY GOOD CENT$ BUDGET FOR THE MONTH OF

_____

ESTIMATED INCOME FOR THE MONTH _____

1) GIVING _____

2) SAVING _____

3) TAXES _____

4) HOUSING _____

   Mortgage/Rent _____

   Water _____

   Electric _____

   Gas _____

   Phone _____

5) TRANSPORTATION _____

   Car payment _____

   Gasoline _____

6) FOOD/HOUSEHOLD _____

7) INSURANCE _____

8) DEBTS _____

9) BELOW BALANCE _____

10) MISC. _____

   Cable _____

   Cell Phone _____

   Subscriptions _____

11) VACATION _____

12) CHRISTMAS _____

13) _____

14) _____

15) ALL OTHER _____

MY GOOD CENT$ BUDGET FOR THE MONTH OF

_____

ESTIMATED INCOME FOR THE MONTH _____

   1) GIVING _____

   2) SAVING _____

   3) TAXES _____

   4) HOUSING _____

      Mortgage/Rent _____

      Water _____

      Electric _____

      Gas _____

      Phone _____

   5) TRANSPORTATION _____

      Car payment _____

      Gasoline _____

   6) FOOD/HOUSEHOLD _____

   7) INSURANCE _____

   8) DEBTS _____

   9) BELOW BALANCE _____

   10) MISC. _____

      Cable _____

      Cell Phone _____

      Subscriptions _____

   11) VACATION _____

   12) CHRISTMAS _____

   13) _____

   14) _____

   15) ALL OTHER _____

MY GOOD CENT$ BUDGET FOR THE MONTH OF

_____

ESTIMATED INCOME FOR THE MONTH _____

    1) GIVING   _____

    2) SAVING   _____

    3) TAXES   _____

    4) HOUSING   _____

        Mortgage/Rent   _____

        Water   _____

        Electric   _____

        Gas   _____

        Phone   _____

    5) TRANSPORTATION _____

        Car payment   _____

        Gasoline   _____

    6) FOOD/HOUSEHOLD _____

    7) INSURANCE   _____

    8) DEBTS   _____

    9) BELOW BALANCE _____

    10) MISC.   _____

        Cable   _____

        Cell Phone   _____

        Subscriptions   _____

    11) VACATION   _____

    12) CHRISTMAS   _____

    13)   _____

    14)   _____

    15) ALL OTHER   _____

MY GOOD CENT$ BUDGET FOR THE MONTH OF

_____

ESTIMATED INCOME FOR THE MONTH _____

1) GIVING   _____

2) SAVING   _____

3) TAXES   _____

4) HOUSING   _____

     Mortgage/Rent   _____

     Water   _____

     Electric   _____

     Gas   _____

     Phone   _____

5) TRANSPORTATION   _____

     Car payment   _____

     Gasoline   _____

6) FOOD/HOUSEHOLD   _____

7) INSURANCE   _____

8) DEBTS   _____

9) BELOW BALANCE   _____

10) MISC.   _____

     Cable   _____

     Cell Phone   _____

     Subscriptions   _____

11) VACATION   _____

12) CHRISTMAS   _____

13)   _____

14)   _____

15) ALL OTHER   _____

ALL OF MY DEBTS AS OF _____

SAVING: SHORT-TERM GOALS (One week to six months)

SAVING: LONG-TERM GOALS (Six months to five years)

SAVING: LIFE GOALS (Five years and beyond)

JOURNAL – MY FIRST YEAR ON THE GOOD CENT\$ BUDGET

_____
_____
_____
_____
_____
_____
_____
_____
_____
_____
_____
_____
_____
_____
_____
_____
_____
_____
_____
_____
_____
_____
_____
_____
_____
_____
_____
_____
_____
_____

JOURNAL – MY FIRST YEAR ON THE GOOD CENT$ BUDGET

JOURNAL – MY FIRST YEAR ON THE GOOD CENT$ BUDGET

JOURNAL – MY FIRST YEAR ON THE GOOD CENT$ BUDGET

JOURNAL – MY FIRST YEAR ON THE GOOD CENT$ BUDGET

_____

_____

_____

_____

_____

_____

_____

_____

_____

_____

_____

_____

_____

_____

_____

_____

_____

_____

_____

_____

_____

_____

_____

_____

_____

_____

_____

_____

_____

JOURNAL – MY FIRST YEAR ON THE GOOD CENT$ BUDGET

_____
_____
_____
_____
_____
_____
_____
_____
_____
_____
_____
_____
_____
_____
_____
_____
_____
_____
_____
_____
_____
_____
_____
_____
_____
_____
_____
_____

JOURNAL – MY FIRST YEAR ON THE GOOD CENT$ BUDGET

_____

_____

_____

_____

_____

_____

_____

_____

_____

_____

_____

_____

_____

_____

_____

_____

_____

_____

_____

_____

_____

_____

_____

_____

_____

_____

_____

_____

_____

_____

_____

_____

JOURNAL – MY FIRST YEAR ON THE GOOD CENT$ BUDGET

JOURNAL – MY FIRST YEAR ON THE GOOD CENT$ BUDGET

_____

_____

_____

_____

_____

_____

_____

_____

_____

_____

_____

_____

_____

_____

_____

_____

_____

_____

_____

_____

_____

_____

_____

_____

_____

_____

_____

_____

_____

JOURNAL – MY FIRST YEAR ON THE GOOD CENT$ BUDGET

JOURNAL – MY FIRST YEAR ON THE GOOD CENT$ BUDGET

_____

_____

_____

_____

_____

_____

_____

_____

_____

_____

_____

_____

_____

_____

_____

_____

_____

_____

_____

_____

_____

_____

_____

_____

_____

_____

_____

_____

_____

JOURNAL – MY FIRST YEAR ON THE GOOD CENT$ BUDGET

CPSIA information can be obtained at www.ICGtesting.com
Printed in the USA
LVOW091804160911

246622LV00005B/132/P